F.J. Olsey

Do Koalas Have Tails?

Bumblebee
Books

A CIP catalogue record for this title is
available from the British Library.

ISBN: 978-1-83934-464-0

Bumblebee Books is an imprint of
Olympia Publishers.

First Published in 2023
Bumblebee Books
Tallis House
2 Tallis Street
London
EC4Y 0AB

Printed in Great Britain

Dedication

I dedicate this book to my children MJ & Xavier.

Daddy loves you.

Do koalas have tails?
I just do not know at all.

It's possible they do, but they are very small.

THEY HAVE REALLY BIG CLAWS
AND LIKE TO CLIMB TREES.

KOALAS HAVE FURRY EARS
AND ENJOY EATING LEAVES.

THESE ARE THINGS EVERYONE CAN SEE.

But do koalas have tails?
Who knows what to believe?

KOALAS DON'T HAVE MUCH ENERGY
AND SPEND MOST OF THE DAY,
ASLEEP IN THE TREES,
WHILE OTHER ANIMALS PLAY.
14

OH!
AND THEY DON'T
DRINK MUCH WATER, NO.

17

MOMMY KOALAS HAVE A POUCH
WHERE THEIR BABY JOEY GROWS.

BUT AS FOR A TAIL,
NOBODY KNOWS.

KOALAS COME IN TWO DIFFERENT COLORS.
BROWN AND GRAY ARE THE SHADES
OF THESE TREE HUGGERS.

AND THERE IS ONLY ONE PLACE
WHERE THEY CALL HOME,
IT'S AUSTRALIA
WHERE THEY FREELY ROAM.

AUSTRALIA

So, do koalas have tails?
I'm still not sure.

But I think they do
it's just covered in fur.

27

About the Author

F.J. Olsey is an aspiring children's book author. His enjoyment of writing evolved after a creative writing course in college, and his passion for writing has been fueled by his two energetic children. A bit of an adventurer, F.J. moved 1200 miles from his home in Michigan to Denver Colorado to explore life. Here he met his remarkable wife Christine and they started a family. Today, F.J. resides with his family & pet tortoise in Colorado. In his free time F.J. enjoys live music, farmer's markets, sandy beaches, zoos and making his children laugh.

Ingram Content Group UK Ltd.
Milton Keynes UK
UKHW051224020723
424339UK00003B/6